Tied In A Knot

Tied In A Knot

✦

Rules For A Successful Marriage

Ken Woodcock

Writers Club Press
New York Lincoln Shanghai

Tied In A Knot
Rules For A Successful Marriage

Writers Club Press
an imprint of iUniverse, Inc.

For information address:
iUniverse, Inc.
2021 Pine Lake Road, Suite 100
Lincoln, NE 68512
www.iuniverse.com

ISBN: 0-595-25366-0 (pbk)
ISBN: 0-595-65126-7 (cloth)

Printed in the United States of America

To my wife, Kay, for giving me forty-five years of happiness and contentment. Without you, this book would not have been possible.

Contents

FOREWORD

So what is this thing the world calls marriage? Webster's Seventh New Collegiate Dictionary defines it thusly:

Marriage (n) the institution whereby men and women are joined in a special kind of social and legal dependence for the purpose of founding and maintaining a family.

Sounds a lot like a legal contract or commitment, does it not? It definitely is not a definition the average person in the United States would think of, when considering a marriage relationship, is it? What about those emotional factors such as love, passion and desire? Aren't they the main reasons men and women really get married? Isn't it that titillating feel of wanting to be close to that special someone constantly, day and night, forevermore? Yes, this is the way the western world has been taught to view and understand marriage, especially here in the United States. We westerners see the marriage rite as an emotional bonding of man and woman, not a legal obligation to foster society. This is not the way it has always been, however, nor is it the way most of the Eastern world looks at matrimony today.

Throughout history, even in this country, the marriage rite has been predominately a method to develop and propagate civilizations. Princes from one country have been betrothed to princesses from foreign countries in order to unite kingdoms and deter wars. King Solomon is perhaps the most extreme example of this custom, having married hundreds of women from surrounding countries, to maintain a peaceful state for his kingdom of Israel. In some countries, even today, the daughter of one family is given to the son of another family for the purpose of uniting those families and propagating the community. These young couples may not even meet until their wedding day, yet they will become husband and wife and be committed to raise and maintain a family, according to the rules and obligations of that society. And, as Webster states, this is socially and legally accepted within that culture.

Whichever view one espouses, the Eastern view where marriages are arranged and the couple is committed to build a family within that culture or, the Western view where a man and a woman choose one another based on a feeling of love to unite and raise a family, there is one thing both sides can agree on. Once a man and a woman become husband and wife, it is not always easy to live happily ever after. Men and women are so totally different in their makeup, both physically and emotionally; it is almost impossible for them to live together for any length of time, without driving one another to the point of insanity. In the United States, the divorce rate for first time marriages is approaching sixty-five percent. That means almost two out of every three of first time marriages in this country fail. Europe and other western countries have similarly high rates of divorce. Is this an indication that the Eastern method of family life is superior to the Western? Not necessarily. Divorce is much easier to obtain in the West as opposed to the East and, in fact, most Eastern cultures do not track divorce ratios, as does the West. Eastern families may be having just as hard a time with marriage; it is just more difficult for them to get out of it.

Shouldn't there be a guideline available to enable a man and a woman to live together as dedicated spouses, without one or both being committed to a sanitarium? I believe that those guidelines are given in the Holy Bible. God, in His infinite wisdom gave us basic rules that, if followed, will allow couples to live happy, dedicated lives with one another. After all, God instituted the first marriage in the Garden of Eden with Adam and Eve, and he earnestly desires that every wedded couple find happiness and contentment within the family.

In the course of this book, I propose to present some of these rules, in an effort to help married couples in understanding their responsibilities and commitments to marriage, and in so doing, possibly make their marriages happier, and their lives more contented. It is my belief, following these guidelines will help regardless of a person's religion, beliefs or cultural background. God's rules as expounded here are not only found in the Holy Bible, but are discussed in other religious writings, such as the Torah and the Koran, an indication that God is not limited to one book or one doctrine. He is God.

1

MAN AND WOMAN

"And the Lord God took the man, and put him into the garden of Eden to dress it and to keep it." (Genesis 2:15)

"And the Lord God said, 'It is not good that the man should be alone, I will make him an help meet for him.'" (Genesis 2:18)

The Garden of Eden must have been an exceedingly beautiful place. In your mind's eye, picture this magnificent spot that God set aside from the rest of the earth, to be a place where he could have fellowship with his creation, man. Enormous, green-frocked trees spread their branches heavenward, bowing under the weight of fruit and nuts of every kind. Their billowing leaves wafted in the cool soothing breeze, overlooking verdant meadows, covered with a kaleidoscope of wild flowers, resplendent in their beauty of every color and design. Clear, bubbling brooks meandered their way through luscious, green covered valleys, gurgling in tranquil sounds of peace and harmony, as the crystal waters passed over the rocks.

Animals of every conceivable size and shape, from the wee titmouse to the gigantic elephants, roamed freely, without fear of predators or other dangers, as they cavorted merrily in the forests and plains. Mighty lions with shaggy manes and wooly lambs were nestled together in the cool grasses to nap together. All manner of beautiful birds flew overhead, unafraid of the foxes and tigers stroll-

ing below them. There was no death or pain, only peace and seren-
ity.

On our thirtieth anniversary, my wife, Kay, and I visited the
island of Maui in Hawaii. After driving the S-shaped Hanna road in
a pouring rain, we reached the National Park, close to Hanna.
Because of the rain, when we arrived, the parking lot was empty, not
another car was in sight. As we pulled the rental car into a parking
space, the rain suddenly ceased and a bright sun burst through the
clouds, revealing a multi-colored rainbow. The moist air was cool
and exceptionally clear.

Entering the park, and being totally alone, we headed to the
seven sacred pools. There we were, my wife and I, surrounded by
the most beautiful place I had ever seen, with not another human
around. A tall waterfall flowed from hundreds, if not thousands, of
feet up at the top of the mountain, and cascaded down into a huge
pool, which overflowed and continued down to the next pool, until
seven pools were filled with the crisp, clear water of the melting
snow from above. Exiting the seventh pool, the water continued
into the turquoise expanse of the Pacific Ocean. Luscious greenery
and brilliant tropical plants provided a botanical wonderland.
Hibiscus and orchids grew freely and in abundance.

This was just a sample of what the Garden of Eden must have
been like. As I gingerly took a dip in the cold waters of the seventh
pool, a brief shower returned, soaking my wife, who had not wished
to go in the water, because she didn't want to get wet. She stood
there drenched, her long blonde hair now straight and sticking to
her cheeks, and any makeup she may have been wearing, washed
away. Uncontrollably, I laughed at her predicament as she pouted

about her misfortune. In this exotic setting, she could not have appeared lovelier. In that instant, she was my Eve.

God placed Adam in the Garden of Eden to dress and keep it. The first work given to man was that of a professional gardener, and Adam was provided with everything he needed to do the job. He had fruits, nuts and vegetables of all kinds for nourishment, a splendid place to lie down and rest when he felt weary, and all the animals to frolic and play with. Plus, he had communion with God daily. What a seemingly wonderful existence. Yet, something was missing in Adam's life, an indescribable lack of a relationship that even God could not provide, because of God's magnificent deity. Adam loved the animals that, one by one, he had named, but unlike Dr. Dolittle, he could not understand them when they mooed, barked or chirped, and they had no idea of his inner feelings and emotions. In all of this vast beauty and wonder, Adam became lonely, and he didn't even know what he was lonely for.

How long Adam tended the garden until Eve came on the scene, no one can know. Was it a million years? A billion? Or merely a week or two? God is not limited by time. Time is a device developed by man to determine history and to schedule his own comings and goings. A day to God may be many of eons of what man counts in time. What is certain is that at some point, God looked at Adam and said, "It is not good that the man should be alone." Let me emphasize this point. It was God who recognized the need in Adam, and He decided to do something about it. It is the same today; God still recognizes man's need and is there to provide for it.

God said, "I will make a help meet for him." Again, as a point of information, Adam did not come to God asking for a woman. He was not crying to be saved from his loneliness. This woman thing was all God's idea. The creation of woman is a testimony to the wisdom, and also to the humor of God. Why couldn't God have just made another man to help Adam with his chores in the garden, and provide someone to fellowship with? If you can still remember your first kiss, or the initial time you took a girl's hand in yours, and can recall the butterflies of your first crush, or remember realizing for the first time in your life, you were in love, the answer to that question is obvious. Oh, the marvelous wisdom of God.

According to the scriptures, God put Adam into a deep sleep, so He could perform an operation on him. While Adam slept, God removed one of his ribs, and then closed the flesh back up around Adam's ribcage. The bone that God used was taken from an area of man that is in his most ticklish spot, an indication that woman was designed to provide man with laughter. Then God took the rib that he removed from Adam and created woman. Isn't it interesting that the woman wasn't made from the dust, as Adam had been, but from a part of the very body of Adam? To be complete again, Adam needed the woman and, likewise, for the woman to be complete, she needed to return to the man. Whereas God spoke the firmament into place, the implication here is that God took his hands and carefully molded the woman into being, making her his final masterpiece.

God then brought the woman to Adam. Imagine for a moment, yourself as Adam, seeing a woman for the very first time. Before you is this creature that stands erect and walks upright like you do. She has features similar to yours, a mouth, two eyes, and ears; yet she is amazingly different. Her long hair flows down her back in billowing curls, her spider-like eyelids flutter when she blinks, and her full mouth tantalizes you as she speaks. You glance down at your body and then back at hers. There are round, fully developed curves head to toe on the woman that your body doesn't possess. You breathlessly turn to God and, in a thankful manner, say, "Good job, God, you have really done a good job." And God looks back knowingly at you with the humor that all wisdom gives him, nods and smiles.

For God did not make woman to be exactly like man, quite the contrary. Adam had no idea what he was getting when Eve appeared for that first time in the garden. God used a different blueprint and cast a mold like none He had ever used before. It was not only her appearance that was different, but also her very nature. I will not delve into those differences at this point, but suffice it to say that books such as, "Men Are From Mars, Women Are From Venus" and plays like, "The Caveman" have been written exploiting those differences. It is these very differences that make the relationship between a man and a woman so exciting and exhilarating. Married couples need to realize these differences and, rather than fight against them, learn to use them to solidify a marriage. Tolerance and understanding are necessary for any type of relationship. Add God's love into the mix and you have the perfect recipe for a long and successful marriage and a lot of fun along the way.

2

MAN SEEKS WOMAN

"Be ye not unequally yoked together with unbelievers." (II Corinthians 6:14)

Finding the right wife or husband is not an easy assignment. The ritual of courtship is filled with traps and snares that can demoralize even the most confident of persons. Libraries are filled with books written about crushes, puppy loves, and affairs that failed, leaving boys and girls, men and women devastated. The dating process, as it is practiced in western society, is definitely one of trial and error. One of our greatest errors, is that we are not looking towards the future when we begin out search for love; instead, we are looking for instant gratification and acceptance in the present. When a young man looks at an attractive woman, he isn't necessarily thinking, "I would sure like to marry her, settle down and raise a family."

What is more than likely running through his head is something along the lines of, "Boy, she's hot, I wonder if I can get her to go out with me?" He, at this point, isn't interested in a long-term relationship, just a chance to meet and know the girl. Little does he understand the indiscriminate aim of Cupid's arrow? Love can strike the heart at any time and in any place, and when it does, the victim is hooked.

Second Corinthians 6:14 states, "Do not be unequally yoked together with unbelievers." The admonition of this scripture is for Christians not to marry non-Christians. The Apostle Paul encourages Christian youth of the first century to seek their spouses within the confines of their faith. Paul is not the first person to advocate a person marrying within his faith. Centuries before Paul, Jewish leaders taught the same message to the young men and women of their day. Many of Israel's biggest problems were caused by Jews' intermarriage with those who worshipped idols and false Gods. In Islam today, if a child decides to marry someone outside of his or her religion, he or she is considered dead, no longer a part of the family.

There is practical reasoning behind this rationale. As has been mentioned earlier, and will be reiterated as we go through this book, men and women are vastly different in their approach to life. Those differences will cause all sorts of disagreements, arguments and dissensions in the normal living together as man and wife. The more common ground a couple possesses, physically, emotionally and spiritually, the better the chance for a long and fulfilling marriage. When serious problems occur, as they eventually will, and a couple can go to their knees in prayer and supplication to the same God, there is a binding effect on that relationship. They will grow stronger in their feelings to one another and to their God.

I have had the pleasure of working with youth for thirty-six years in three states. I have spoken at youth camps, churches and youth rallies, and have taught seminars on working with youth. My message to Christian young people has always been the same, when you date; date other Christians. Of course, I always get flack and criticism from some of the youth, who cannot see the hidden dangers in dating outside their faith.

One of our youth, a girl named Betty, liked a boy and began bringing him to our church activities in South Carolina. Bobby was a nice kid, but he had a drinking problem and constantly stayed in trouble with his parents. Though he heard the Gospel message and saw how other kids had been changed by it, he never stepped out on faith to make a personal commitment.

After graduation, Betty came to me one evening and told me she and Bobby had decided to get married. I gave my usual speech about uniting with a non-Christian, and the problems that could be encountered. She was confident, as most people in this situation usually are, that she could get him to change, and make a decision after they were married. Reluctantly, I wished her luck and prayed with her. I attended their wedding and kept in touch with them until I moved to Virginia. They ran into financial difficulty after having two children, and Bobby began drinking heavily. He became abusive and beat Betty, one time putting her in the hospital. The marriage ended in divorce.

A similar situation occurred when I was Youth Director at a church in Louisiana. Mary fell in love with a young man named Mark. Mark, at the time, was an architectural student at LSU. Mark was a sharp, handsome young man, fun to be around. He was Catholic. The two sat down with me one day and discussed their plans for getting married, as soon as Mark graduated. We discussed the differences in their faiths. Now I happen to believe a person can be Catholic and be a Christian, but there are some strong differences between orthodox Catholicism and Baptist belief. Mary and Mark assured me they could work through any religious problems that may arise in the future..

For eight years, Mary and Mark had an ideal marriage. Mark worked at a major architectural firm and Mary was a schoolteacher. When their oldest son reached an age to begin school, the problems occurred. Mark wanted him educated in a Catholic parochial school and Mary wanted him to go to public school. Mark also wanted their son to begin attending Catholic Mass, which Mary fought tooth and nail. The conflict could not be resolved and ended in a bitter separation and eventually, divorce.

Christians are not exempted from financial problems, or any other calamities that humans face. But when a married couple is of one accord in their spiritual belief, they have a common source to seek for inner strength and guidance. They can go to one God, united in the knowledge that God is going to do what is best for them, not only as individuals, but as a couple. What a wonderful feeling to hold the hand of the woman you love, and pray to a God you both worship.

When I met my wife, I had no idea that she would be the girl I would spend the majority of my life with. Many people talk about love at first sight and I think that is great, but it did not happen for me that way. At eighteen, a high school senior and leader of my church's youth group, I was cocky and arrogant. At the time, I did not see myself as that way, but in retrospect, I must be honest.

Kay walked into the Richmond Arena skating rink with several girls, who were members of my church youth group, who lived on the south side of Richmond. She instantly caught my eye. Tall, with blue eyes, she was blonde and shapely. I knew right away, I wanted to meet this new girl and get to know her. With my older married brother by my side, I skated over to the group of girls.

"Hey, Beverly, how about introducing me to your friend?" I asked a member of the group that I knew.

Making a production of the whole thing, Beverly waved her hand in introducing my brother Keith and I to Kay. Kay nodded, mentioned that she was pleased to meet us, and politely reached to shake my hand. As I took her hand in mine, I noticed how cold her long, slender fingers were. Her eyes focused on the floor instead of me, as we clasped in the polite handshake.

Using my most romantic voice, I said, "You sure are cute, maybe we should get together sometime."

"I don't think so," she replied, coyly lifting her eyes to meet mine. Then she turned and walked away.

Throughout the remainder of the evening, I kept looking for her in the crowd that encircled the skating floor. I tried to skate especially well, hoping to impress her with my abilities on the floor, and every once in a while, I would catch the sight of the blonde hair and notice her blue eyes watching me. But I never got another chance to talk to her that night. Keith needled me all the way home about what a great lover I was, but I just replied, confidently, "Don't worry, big brother, she'll call me before the week is over."

I am not sure I really believed she would call, but sure enough, on the Wednesday night after the skating party, the phone in my living room rang. It was Kay, who claimed Beverly and the rest of the girls had put her up to making the call, a story I never believed. So I began dating Kay, but with no intention of becoming serious. In fact, I honestly thought at the time, I was in love with someone else.

As we began to learn each other's likes and dislikes, and our attitudes toward life, my feelings for her grew stronger and stronger, without me even being aware of it happening. It took a brief breakup for me to realize that I indeed was in love with this girl with the long blonde hair and blue eyes.

When I had first starting dating Kay, I never worried about her spiritual beliefs or whether she attended church, but now, deep in love, these things mattered. Of course, by that time, it would have been too late. I was in love. I would probably have married her even if she had been into witchcraft. My story easily could have ended up similar to that of Betty or Mary's, but by the grace of God, Kay had accepted Christ and been baptized in a local Baptist church. I am sure the prayers of a loving mother helped lead me to the right woman for marriage, because I would never have been able to do it on my own.

There have been divorces on both sides of our family. My brother married twice with both ending in divorce and Kay's three sisters have had multiple marriages, all ending in divorce. Many of our friends are divorced. We are no different from them, except we have tried to stay true to the Word of God. We have continued to worship as a couple, and we have lived by the rules set forth in the Bible for marital relationships. When there were problems or losses, we were able to console one another in the knowledge that God gives us peace and strength. This has sustained us through forty-five years. It will sustain any couple that follows God's rules.

So what if you find yourself wed to a person who worships differently? Do you give up and say this marriage can't work. Of course not! As God ordained the union of Adam and Eve in the garden, he also ordains and sanctions all marriages. God does not wish to see any marriage or family end in divorce. In fact, God did not institute divorce; it was man who came up with the idea, an idea that continues to destroy our society today by breaking up families and leaving children confused and feeling unwanted.

Having the same religion is very important, but it is not the only thing that makes a marriage. Many Christian marriages have ended in divorce. Why? Without trying to be judgmental, I believe it is because those involved have not adhered completely to the guidelines that God has given us. It is my belief that when a couple follows the guidelines given in the Bible, divorce is impossible. With that said, I must admit that because of pride, greed and other basic aspects of human nature, that following the guidelines can be very difficult at times. It is for this reason, that daily we need to go to our knees and ask God for His help.

The more things a couple have in common, the better their chance for a successful and blissful life together. Culture, economic status and similar interests play a big part in keeping a man and woman satisfied with one another. Yet, none of these guarantee a happy relationship either. In every human enterprise, whether it is business, governmental or social, there must be rules or laws to live by. When people follow the rules, society works, but when the rules are broken, society suffers. It is the same with a marriage. God has given us rules; all we have to do is obey them.

As mentioned at the beginning of this chapter, finding the right spouse is not an easy assignment. Why, after all the hard work involved, would someone ever want to let her get away? In the song, "Some Enchanted Evening" from "South Pacific", there is a line that says, "Once you have found her, never let her go." Learn God's rules, apply them to your marriage and you will never have to let her go.

3

BREAKING THE APRON STRINGS

"Therefore shall a man leave his father and his mother, and shall cleave unto his wife: and they shall be one flesh." (Genesis 2:24)

A newborn baby is delivered into the world. This miraculous creation of God is immediately placed in the loving arms of his or her mother. She tenderly takes the infant, holding him close to her bosom, and hums a favorite melody sweetly to him. With soft, warm hands and gentle fingers, the mother caresses the baby's cheek and plays with his tiny strands of hair. From the very instant after birth, a newborn child begins building an attachment to its' mother. For many weeks, the child is dependent on the mother for every conceivable need, its' nourishment, its' health and its' feeling of belonging and being loved. In a proper family setting, the attachment grows and prospers, and this is good.

Very soon after delivery, the child feels heavier, rougher hands picking her up and cradling her awkwardly in hairy arms. The voice that the child hears is deeper, more resonant, yet still with a loving tone. The babe is introduced to the father, who will be a protector, a playmate, an instructor and a friend. As the years past, the child strengthens and grows, rolling over, crawling and taking that first step. She learns from her mother how to cook, sew and shop or he is taught sports and camping from a caring dad. They are a family and have developed a binding relationship between child and parents.

"I want to marry my mom," little Johnny says at age five, not understanding the complexities of adult life, but knowing who, in his eyes, is the best cook, homemaker and best looking girl in the whole wide world.

Jenny, approaching ten and just learning about boys, tells her friend that, when she marries, she wants a man exactly like her dad. In her eyes, he is the most handsome, strongest and most caring person in the universe.

Then, between the ages of eleven and fourteen, an amazing transition takes place in these children, as they begin to develop into adulthood. A thing psychologists call adolescence or puberty. All the enzymes, atoms, molecules and ions in their bodies go haywire and they start looking at males and females of the opposite sex, rather than their parents. In some Eastern cultures, it is at this age one family may offer a daughter to be wed to another families' son. In India, Mahatma Gandhi's wife was betrothed to him when she was twelve, and they were wed at the age of thirteen.

An eagle will feed and tend her young until their feathers are fully developed and their bodies and wings have begun to spread and grow strong. Then she will gently nudge the tottering eaglet over the edge of the nest, until the small creature falls into the nothingness of space below it. Even though the mother eagle soars nearby, ever ready to swoop down and catch the eaglet if needed, the young bird, unknowing, spreads its' wings in an effort to remain airborne. And almost always, the young eagle is successful, as it catches the wind and finds itself soaring high above the green earth below and rising into an azure blue sky.

The young eagle will not return to the nest or its' mother, but fly away to seek a life of its' own. And the mother eagle feels no remorse. Her job of raising the eaglet is complete and she goes on with her life.

A lioness nurses her cub and protects him from any predators that might have an eye to harm him. She plays with the cub and teaches him the ways of the wilds in which he must live, tenderly pressing him to her side at night. But when the young lion grows to be an adult, he finds that he must leave the pride, for there can be only one male lion to rule the group. So the younger lion slips into the jungle, where he will find a mate and start his own pride. And the mother goes and again lies with her mate, her King of the Jungle, and, like the eagle, feels no remorse.

And so it is in almost all of nature, when the young are grown, they leave their families to begin life on their own. Neither the parents, nor the offspring grieve or attempt to reassemble as a family. The major exception is the human race. For some reason, we Homo sapiens, especially the mothers, have a difficult time giving up their offspring, and maintain a graving desire to keep their children close to them. Having a close relationship with parents is not necessarily a bad thing, but when that relationship interferes with the relationship between a man and his wife, it can become bad.

There was a letter in the newspaper recently, written to "Dear Abby" from a young man who was planning to get married. He was concerned that his mother wanted to go on the honeymoon with he and his new bride. Not only did she want to come along, but she also thought it would be a good idea for all the young groom's close relatives to come, so it could be a family affair, a vacation of sorts where they could all be together. The young man did not want to hurt his mother's feelings, but felt he and his bride should have that honeymoon time alone together. He asked Abby for advice on how to approach his mother on the subject.

Now you may think this is unusual, farfetched and even a little ridiculous, and I have a tendency to agree with you, at least on the ridiculous part. But, it is neither as unusual nor farfetched as it may seem. Some parents do travel with their honeymooning children. I talked to a couple that went on a cruise for their honeymoon and say they had a wonderful time with their parents along. The difference between this couple and the man writing to "Dear Abby", is that they agreed to the parents joining them. It was the couples' decision to invite his parents.

So what did Abby say? She advised the young man to tell his mother that he loved her deeply, but he felt he needed to be alone with his new wife on the honeymoon. He could offer to go somewhere on vacation with the family at a later date. I hope it worked out for the young groom.

I have a friend who is in his thirties. He lives with his mother. She is neither an invalid nor a hardship case. The friend is deeply in love with a young woman, who he has been engaged to for many years. His mother does not want him to get married and leave her alone. As long as she is alive, he probably never will. Obviously, the ties to his mother are stronger than the feelings he has for the woman. A family that could be, most likely will not be, at least for a considerable time.

Genesis 2:24 says, *"A man shall leave his father and mother and cleave to his wife."* This is God's second rule for making a marriage work, and the verse also applies to a woman, who must cleave to her husband. Once the decision has been made to become husband and wife, a clean break must be made with the past. This doesn't mean we stop loving our parents and turn our backs on them, far from it. What it does mean is that when we say, "I do" at the altar, we center our emotional and physical being on our spouse. We become united. As the Bible puts it, "they shall be one flesh". The man is now dependent on the woman and the woman is dependent on the man. They are no longer dependent on their parents to meet their needs, but rely totally on one another under the direction of God's will.

"Becoming one flesh," is more than a physical union between two individuals. It is also bonding together emotionally and spiritually. It is becoming of one accord. The two develop an oneness by talking and listening to each other, and communicating together to God. The term "soul mates" is no longer an exaggeration, but a reality.

The breaking of any rules can bring devastating consequences. Two of my very close friends were married soon after graduating from high school. The wife came from a fairly well to do family, which had given her almost everything she ever asked for. Her husband came from a stable, but poorer background, one with pride and good family values.

The girl's father did not really approve of the future son-in-law, but because he loved his daughter, he agreed to accept her choice of a husband. When the couple decided to build a home, they found they could not afford anything near what the wife had grown accustomed to living in. Her father offered to put a large down payment on a house much larger than the husband could afford, on the condition that the couple would build close to them. The husband did not want to rely on his father-in-laws' money, but rather, felt he should be responsible for providing for his wife. However, after much discussion and deliberation, he let his wife convince him that it would be foolish not to accept this tremendous offer from her father.

They purchased and moved into a house less than a block from her father and mother. They didn't have a chance. The wife never broke the apron strings, which in this case, were tied to her father. Whenever there were arguments or dissensions, the wife could run home to daddy for solace. Slowly, the husband began to lose his self-esteem. Over the years and after four children, the marriage gradually dissolved, ending in divorce. Everyone involved in this situation were Christians. They all were aware of the teachings in Genesis. I am sure the girls' father believed he was doing what was best for his daughter. There may be times when, like the eagle, parents need to give their children a little nudge to get them away from the nest.

Please don't misinterpret what is written here. There is not a thing wrong with parents at times helping their children financially, or in any other way. What is wrong is to use that financial aid to manipulate and try keeping the child under the parents' wing.

When my wife and I married, we rented an apartment just three blocks from my mother-in-law. It was only natural that my wife spent a lot of time back in her old home. She was still as much living as her mother's daughter as she was as my wife. The apron strings were loosened, but not released. To make matters worst, I lost my job and we were forced to move in with my mother-in-law. I was with my wife's family in her family's home. Not having a job caused my self-esteem to drop, and I didn't want to rely on my in-laws for support. The atmosphere was not conducive for us to become a close couple. At a time when I should have turned to God for help, I began drinking and stopped going to church altogether. Without going into any detail here, I'll just say those two years were the worst of my married life.

After about three months, I found a job. We saved our money and put a down payment on a nice three-bedroom home. We started attending church again, but were not very active. Even though we had moved, my wife still relied on her mother to take her almost everywhere, since she could not drive. She was still tied to and somewhat dependent on her mother. We were not growing as a couple as we should, emotionally or spiritually.

I firmly believe God has a master plan for each of us. In his infinite wisdom, he arranged for me to get transferred to Louisiana. Over a thousand miles away from family and friends, we had to learn to depend on each other, and we also began to depend more on God's direction. Kay got her driver's license. She had always been shy and reserved, but now she began talking to and meeting new people. We joined a local church, where I began my ministry with young people and Kay starting working in the church nursery. Our entire outlook on life changed as we started to truly become of one flesh. The apron strings were finally broken.

Gods' instruction is for a man to leave his mother and father, not to abandon them. The commandment to "honor your mother and father" is still in place. The love one has for his mother and father does not end when he weds. When the marriage vows are taken, the man is no longer subjected to or dependent upon his parents, but places his dependency on his wife and becomes subjected to her desires, but he still has a responsibility to his parents. A stable relationship is desirable between both spouses and their parents. The primary priority for a man, however, is to his wife.

4

WHO'S THE BOSS?

"Wives, submit yourselves unto your own husbands, as unto the Lord. For the husband is the head of the wife, even as Christ is the head of the church." Ephesians 5:22,23

As I begin to type this chapter, I can picture some women's lib advocate, as she begins to read. She is dressed a in solid-color business suit, with her hair pulled back in a tight bun. She stares at the page through dark rimmed glasses. Her back is straight in the chair, with her legs pressed tightly together. She is thinking, "Here we go again. Another male chauvinist, telling me how to bow down and worship my husband, along with the rest of male Dom."

Let me start by emphasizing two points:

1. These are not my words. They are the words of the Apostle Paul taken from The Holy Bible.

2. They have absolutely nothing to do with women's rights, equal pay for equal work or the superiority of the sexes.

Paul is writing to Christian husbands and wives in Ephesus, instructing them on methods to maintain a happy marital relationship and a closer walk with their Savior, Jesus Christ. Moreover, it is not only Paul, but also the inspiration of the Holy Spirit speaking through his writing. As far as we know, Paul was not married. Yet, as an apostle, he was given insight into the many facets of everyday living. He knew what God expected of husbands and wives, and the interrelationship of family life.

"Wives, submit yourselves to your own husbands." This idea of submitting, unfortunately, has been given a negative connotation in today's society. Many interpret the word "submit" to mean, "give away all your rights and allow someone to stomp all over you, or to push you around." Actually, we submit ourselves constantly in our daily lives, without even thinking about it. Yesterday, I mailed my Federal income tax return. I had to fork over more than six hundred dollars, even though the IRS had withdrawn taxes from my checks all year. I was not real happy about having to do this, but I submitted to the taxation laws of the United States. Why? Because I am a citizen of the United States, I support our government.

Have you ever stopped at a red light? Did it occur to you that you were submitting to a traffic law? Probably not, but you were. When was the last time you attended a movie or a sporting event? Did you purchase a ticket? You submitted to the rules of the cinema or stadium where the event was held. They may have even directed you to sit in a specific seat, which you did. Go to a mall before it opens and you cannot get into the stores. Why? Because, you must submit yourself to the mall's operating hours. The list could go on and on, but I think you get the picture. In nearly every thing we do, there is some type of submission involved, and the majority of it is imposed on us.

Paul, however, is asking wives to voluntarily submit themselves to their husbands. Why? Because this is another of God's rules for a happy marriage. It goes hand in hand with cleaving to her husband. If my friend in Chapter Three had submitted to her husband instead of relying on her father's money, their marriage may have survived.

So what does submitting in this context mean? It means deferring to the will and opinions of your husband. It means doing everything possible to meet his needs, physically, emotionally and spiritually. It means, in matters of the home, pushing your husband into the lime-light and humbly staying in the shadows yourself. This does not mean that a wife cannot have her own opinions and the right to voice them, just that she be willing to defer to her husband, if neces-sary. God does not force a wife to submit to her husband, no more than He forces a person to believe in Him. The wife makes the choice to submit of her own free will. God's rules are given to help us have a better life, He knows they will work. We can either accept them or reject them.

Paul goes on to say, that the reason a wife should do this, is because the husband is the head of the wife, even as Christ is the head of the church. Paul's letter is written to Christian couples that have a mutual understanding of the Lordship of Jesus, so wives, hearing these words, are aware of their duty as pertaining to God's will. God's rule is that the husband be the head of the home and family. It is not an arguable point. A wife may stomp her feet, rant and rave, and declare the rule to be unfair, but nothing changes. To maintain a long, happy, and successful marriage, this rule must be followed. I could scream that the government is charging me too much for taxes, and sometimes I do, but should I stop paying the IRS promptly, my happiness in being a United States citizen could change.

Why did God make man the head? Man was made first. God gave him the responsibility to name all the animals and tend the garden. Woman was made from man, an extension of his very body. Isn't it only reasonable that God kept man in charge? Some theologians claim the reason man was put at the head of the wife is because woman initiated original sin. Nothing could be farther from the truth. Adam was the head of Eve before sin entered into the picture. Like the animals, he named her, calling her woman. God gave Adam a responsibility for caring for Eve. Husbands today, continue to have a responsibility to care for their wives.

What is the need for having a head of the family? In any organization, there must be someone at the top, someone to go to when problems arise. A family is an organization, and the husband has the responsibility to be the head of that organization, and it is an awesome responsibility indeed. That responsibility includes more that just providing material comforts. It includes teaching morals and spiritual values to the children. It means living a Godly example for the family to follow. Unfortunately, many husbands shirk these leadership responsibilities, leaving the wife to pick up the slack. When this happens, the wife begins acting like the head of the house, making it difficult for her to be the submissive wife she is supposed to be.

Each family member has certain abilities and talents that can be used to make the family stronger. A husband, as head of the house, must recognize those qualities and see that they are utilized properly. The husband has to manage his home similar to someone running a business. Normally, women are thought of as homemakers, doing the housework and taking care of the children, but if the wife's forte is in finances, she should be handling the family's money. Allowing a wife to use her God given talents in family matters is beneficial to all concerned. The husband must not, however, relinquish the leadership responsibility God has placed upon him.

Being the head of the wife does not give the husband the right to be a dictator or tyrant, expecting his spouse to wait on him hand and foot. It does not allow him to abuse or frustrate her in any way. Paul did not end his letter to the Ephesians at verse 23. Let's take a look at what Paul says in verse 25 of Chapter 5.

"Husbands, love your wives, even as Christ also loved the church, and gave himself for it."

So, then, if a husband is to expect his wife to be submissive, as Paul asked in verse 22, then he must be willing to do what Paul states in verse 25. We are not talking here about the emotional, erotic love that western society thinks about between a man and a woman. No, this love goes much deeper, it is the love that Christ had for the church.

Jesus Christ gave up his position in heaven at the right hand of God, to come to earth and be born in a lowly stable. Throughout his life, He was a servant to the masses around Him. He ministered to their every need, healing them when they were sick, and feeding them when they were hungry. Similarly, a husband should minister to the needs of his wife, comforting her when she is feeling poorly and providing food and shelter for her. Jesus exemplified humility when He bowed down and washed the disciples feet. A good husband should humble himself before his wife, never lord himself over her.

Jesus carried love to extreme limits. He was willing to be ridiculed, beaten and crucified on a cruel Roman cross for the sake of the church. "Greater love has no man, that he is willing to lay down his life for a friend." Chances are you will never have to give your life to save your wife's, but God's rule is that you love her enough that you would be willing to do so. When a husband shows the love of Christ to his wife, it becomes easy for her to submit to his will and direction for the family. When a couple is following God's rules, happiness and contentment permeate every aspect of their family life. A wife's submission and a husband's Christ-like love go like a hand in a glove to ensure an effective, happy marriage.

5

WHAT IS THIS LOVE?

"Nevertheless let every one of you in particular so love his wife even as himself; and the wife see that she reverence her husband." Ephesians 5:33

Paul writes to the husbands in the church at Ephesus, instructing every one of them to love his wife as he loves his own self. How interesting? What do you think of yourself? Do you intentionally inflict pain on yourself? Probably not, it hurts. When you are hungry, do you get something good to eat? Thirsty, do you make yourself a cold drink? More than likely, you do, because you want to take care of your body. It probably hasn't been long since you bought something nice to wear, even though you already have a closet full to the brim of suits, shirts and ties. You want your body dressed nice, don't you? Do you sometimes catch yourself glancing in the mirror to admire how you appear? If we are honest, we will all have to admit that we think a lot of ourselves.

When I was a teenager in the fifties, I spent hours in front of a mirror combing my hair. In those days, we wore something that was called a "ducktail". The hair was combed back on the side; meeting in the back in what more or less resembled a duck's rear end. I used pink pomade to hold it in place. Every hair had to be just right, because once it was finished; it pretty much stayed that way all day.

I could play an entire basketball game and not get a single hair out of place. I wanted to look my best, and to some extent, still do.

Husbands, according to this scripture, you are to love your wife as you love yourself. Never do anything to hurt her, provide for her physical needs and clothing, and make sure she looks and feels her best, by encouraging and complimenting the things she does. It is interesting that Paul never asks the wife to love her husband. Earlier, in verse 22, he tells her to submit to the husband, and here he tells her to reverence him. Maybe Paul feels that is what we husbands really need, to be put up on a pedestal and reverenced.. What else is involved in this love we are supposed to show to our wives?

We have been overwhelmed by the entertainment and marketing industries, showing and telling us in movies, magazines, books and television soap operas just what love is. The wide screen depicts men and women; not necessarily married, pulling off their clothes and rushing into bedrooms, or any room available, to indulge in what the entertainment industry tells us is supposed to be love. Nude bodies are shown clasped together rolling on a bed, a floor, or perhaps in a green meadow, experiencing sheer ecstasy and fulfillment. There is passion, emotion and exhilaration beyond belief.

Daily soaps show the stars changing partners on a monthly basis, as they fall in and out of love with scheduled regularity. Each affair is more exciting, and deeply thought provoking than the one before. It is no wonder that viewers hooked on these types of programs begin to feel there is something missing in their own marriage.

Romance novels are the number one selling genre of literature in the United States today. Most are written by women, read by women, and each of the stories published are remarkably similar. Whether the story is a mystery, historical fiction, or straight drama, the plot is always essentially the same. An average woman is placed in an unusual circumstance where she meets, and is swept off her feet by a handsome stranger. There is always passion, emotion and, usually sex.

Advertisers have not been reluctant to pick up on this sexual phenomenon.

They specialize in showing beautiful women and handsome men in the barest of attire, in an effort to sell merchandise, from new cars to breakfast cereals. Marketers use our desire for love and fulfillment to push every product available, hiring lovely models and winsome movie stars to entice the avid viewers and readers. Use the proper deodorant, hairspray or aftershave, and the opposite sex will be automatically drawn to us, we are told. Drink the right cola or cater to the right business establishments and true love will definitely come your way.

In all these cases, love is shown as passion, excitement, attraction and eroticism. Paul's words inform us, this is not what true love is. Don't misunderstand, there is nothing inherently wrong with sex when used in its' proper context, in the bond of matrimony, and that item will be discussed in the next chapter. Please don't jump ahead. But, for now I want to look at what love, as God designed it, really is.

It would be presumptuous on my part to develop my own definition of love, when Paul has defined it so well in what has come to be known as the love chapter of the Bible, in I Corinthians, chapter thirteen. In verses four through eight, Paul describes love thusly:

"Love is patient, love is kind. It does not envy, it does not boast, it is not proud. It is not rude, it is not self-seeking, it is not easily angered, it keeps no record of wrongs. Love does not delight in evil but rejoices with

the truth. It always protects, always trusts, Always hopes, always perseveres. Love never fails." New International Version translation.

You have no doubt heard the saying, "Patience is a virtue." In the marital relationship, it is more than a virtue; it is an act of love. It is not by chance that Paul listed patience first in his description of love. For anyone who has been married more than a week, it is easy to understand just how quickly we can become impatient with our spouse, and how quickly our impatience can cause an argument or hard feelings.

Take the example of a young couple that is celebrating their first wedding anniversary. The husband, wanting to do something special for the occasion, has purchased expensive tickets for a play his wife particularly likes. He is ready, dressed immaculately in a tuxedo, and waiting in the living room for his wife. Time passes, it is getting late. He begins to fidget, glancing at his watch every two minutes, as he paces back and forth across the floor..

"Would you please hurry up, the show starts at eight." He yells.

"I'll just be a minute," she replies.

He begins to think about the sixty-five dollars each he has paid for the tickets, and becomes agitated because they are going to miss the opening curtain. Somehow, missing a few minutes of the play has become more important to him than his original intent of pleasing his wife. He is impatient. By the time she is ready, he is in a bad mood, which carries through the entire evening, ruining what could have been a beautiful relationally bonding experience for the couple. Instead, he winds up pouting about being late and she feels hurt. His impatience has destroyed the perfect evening he set out to provide for his wife.

If it wasn't evident before the wedding, it registers soon after, that men and women work on entirely different schedules when it comes to time. A man can get up, shower, shave, eat breakfast and head to work in half an hour. Not so with a woman. She has at least a hundred things that, according to her, absolutely must be done. All of which takes time. When a man calls a friend, the conversation is usually over in five minutes. A woman calling a friend, could easily talk for two hours or better. I have learned when my wife says, "I'll only be a couple of minutes," she will be ready in about a half hour to forty-five minutes. "Just a little while," is considerably longer.

It is not that either is right or wrong, it is just that man and woman are inherently different in the way they think, because God made us that way. Learning patience is a way of showing love to your wife, so it is incumbent, as a husband, that you do so. Striving for patience is not easy. It takes discipline, but it is well worth the effort. For many years, I was very impatient with my wife when it came to shopping. Like most men, I like to go into a store, find what I want and leave. If the store doesn't have what I am looking for, I exit to find the item somewhere else. That is not how my wife shops.

When my wife enters a store, she must look at literally every item, even if she has come for one particular item. It matters not that she was in the very same establishment the day before, and business don't normally change their stock daily, she still must cover every item or, in her mind, the shopping trip has not been completed. Soldiers in the Turkish army have a custom. If their sword is taken from its' scabbard, it cannot be returned without drawing blood. My wife has a similar custom. If she goes into a store, she must buy something before leaving, even if it is something she doesn't need. It is a ritual thing.

In all honesty, I must admit that I avoid going shopping with my wife as much as possible, but when I do, I practice patience. Inevitably, we end up shopping together when we are on vacation. I follow her around, letting her ogle and fondle the wares and merchandise for hours at the time. Sometimes my legs ache and I feel like I have been on a twelve-mile hike. I do it, not because I am crazy, but I know that it is something that makes her happy, and my being patient with her is a way to show my love.

Next, Paul says, "Love is kind." Webster describes the meaning of kind as, *affectionate, loving, a sympathetic nature, gentle and agreeable.* Wow! What a perfect list to characterize true love in a marriage. Remember when you were dating? You were as affectionate and loving as a person could get. You held her hand and placed your arm around her shoulder. You couldn't get close enough in those days and you never wanted to leave her presence. Neither of you needed to say a word, just being together was sufficient. You do remember, don't you?

Ten years after the "I do's" have been said, nothing should change, even twenty, thirty, forty or fifty years later. "But, Ken, be realistic," you may be thinking. "Things change. We have children now, there are bills to pay, I travel a lot and work long hours. I don't have time for that type of thing anymore." Didn't the scripture say, "Love your wife as you love yourself?" Do you find time to eat and drink? How about working out to keep the old body in shape? Took in a good ball game recently? I bet you find time for golf, if that's your bag.

Just how much time does it take to be affectionate? To hold her hand? To brush her hair? To put your arms around her and whisper, "I love you?" Not much time at all.

Having a sympathetic nature involves listening to your wife when she has a problem or concerns, or just happens to be feeling down. Sometimes, we husbands have no inkling what is causing our wife to be upset. The smallest thing can send a woman into a torrent of tears, and she needs to have someone to share that sorrow with.

Early in my marriage, I came home from work one afternoon to find my wife lying on our bed in tears. Normally, at this time she would have supper on the table. Not this day, there were no plates on the table, and no aromas of cooking filling the kitchen. She was about as upset as a person could be. I was convinced that someone in the family had died or been seriously injured. I placed my hand on her shoulder, and lovingly asked what was wrong.

"Marilyn died," she explained.

"Oh, honey, I'm so sorry," I said, in my most sympathetic voice. "Who is Marilyn?"

"Mike's wife," she replied, looking at me incredulously, as if I should have known.

"Oh." I paused, thought a minute, and then continued, "Who is Mike?"

"He's the police detective on 'The Edge of Night'. They're the main characters."

"You mean on television?" As any ignorant husband, who knows no better, I added, "But, honey, they're not real, they are just acting."

I might as well have slapped her. She pulled away from me and dropped her head on the pillow. Then she said, "Well, they are real to me."

I lay beside her, placing my arm tenderly around her shoulder, trying my best to console her. I was sympathetic, although somewhat confused. It is not important that we know why our spouse is upset. Chances are we will never understand them. In fact, I am quite sure of it. What is important is that we are willing to listen, that is what they need. Being gentle and agreeable doesn't hurt, either.

Real love does not envy. A husband should not become jealous of his wife's achievements, rather he should support her and push her towards the goals she is seeking. We live in a society where women have the same opportunity in the work place that men have. In the past, a husband worked and brought in the family income. It is not uncommon now for a wife to earn much more than her husband. Some men may resent this and develop a feeling of inadequacy, which kindles problems in the marriage relationship. When a husband loves his wife the way God expects him to, he rejoices in her successes. A couple living in accordance with God's rules have no reason for envy.

Love is neither boastful nor proud. A successful spouse does not brag about the great things he or she has achieved and lord it over the other spouse. The husband may be the head of the house, but he does not wear any crown.

There is always an inherent risk in being overly successful. Wealth and fame can easily go to a person's head, and they can begin to feel they are better than the person they married. How often have you heard of a singer, actress or even a preacher, who proclaim to be Christian, become popular and wealthy. With their busy schedules, they have little time for the wife or husband. Very soon, their marriage deteriorates and dissolves into divorce. What happened? They broke one of God's rules. They became proud and puffed up, thinking more of self than mate. The love God asks us to show keeps our perspective where is should be. Pride is self-centered and egotistical. Love is centered on an object of affection, your spouse.

Love is not rude. When you were dating, I am sure you always used your best manners around your prospective bride. You were attempting to make a good impression, not only on her, but also on her parents and friends. Maybe you even opened doors and pulled out chairs for her, although I understand this is considered to be old-fashioned by today's standards. Being polite is still a way of showing love to your wife; it is one way that love is displayed in action. Love would never do anything to embarrass a spouse.

Love is not self-seeking. A husband does not manipulate his wife for his own pleasure. Just the opposite is true. A husband shows his love by doing those things that give his wife pleasure. When I was a young man, an elderly gentleman, who had been married for many years told me, "When the wife is happy, I am happy." Live by God's rules and everyone wins.

Love is not easily angered. This one strikes home hard to me. I have never physically hit my wife or abused her in any way, but I cannot count the times she has made me mad about something. You know the type of thing I'm talking about, those little quirks that seem to irritate you and get under your skin. For instance, whenever I can't find an item, I ask my wife where it is. She invariably tells me where to look, which I do. It's never there. After I tear everything apart searching, she will say, "Oh, I forgot. I put it in such and such a place." Thank God, I don't keep a gun in the house.

Here's another example. We are driving down the highway sixty to seventy miles an hour, and I ask her to check the map to find out where we should pull off. Immediately upon passing an interchange, she will coyly remark, "We should have turned there." Or, better yet, she tells me to turn and it's the wrong place, so we have to drive ten extra miles to find a place to turn around. Admittedly, these are small things, and there is another one hundred or so more like them, and they all irritate me. When you love, you should not get mad easily. This is one that I must continue to work on.

It keeps no record of wrongs. This love we are to show to our spouses is continually forgiving. You and your wife are human. There are times when there will be mistakes made, some more serious than others. A marriage cannot survive without forgiveness. Like we all need forgiveness for sins to be right with God, we also need forgiveness of our mistakes to be right with our spouse. Not only must we forgive, we must forget. It is not enough to say, "I will forgive, but I will keep a log book of transgressions." Paul says love keeps no record of wrongs. Once forgiven, it is like they never happened.

Very early in my marriage I made a mistake of gigantic proportions. I was unfaithful. No excuses offered. I was wrong and I know it. My wife had every right to leave me. I needed forgiveness and she gave it, and in over forty years of marriage, she has never brought it up. It is as if it never happened. That kind of forgiveness is the love God wants us to show.

Verse seven says, "It (love) always protects, always trusts, always hopes, always perseveres." The word "always" is used each time.

Love is constantly protecting, trusting, hoping and persevering; it is not a part-time endeavor. This is what love really is. This is how God expects a husband and a wife to love one another.

6

SEX IN MARRIAGE ONLY

"So God created man in his own image, in the image of God created he him, male and female created he them. And God blessed them, and God said unto them, Be fruitful and multiply and replenish the earth." Genesis 1:27,28

"And they were both naked, the man and his wife, and were not ashamed." Genesis 2:25

Contrary to what many people believe, the Bible does not shy away from the subject of sex. In fact, just the opposite is true. The scriptures fully address every aspect of man's sensuality, from the union of a man and woman in Holy matrimony, to acts of perversion, such as homosexuality, and everything in between. An entire book could be written, and maybe already has, on just what the Bible says about sex. Scripture gives clear guidance concerning the proper use of sex within the confines of marriage, and also the detrimental consequences of its' use outside of wedlock.

God created humans with a tremendous sex drive and, outside of the tongue; it is the hardest thing we have to control. In the Garden of Eden, God blessed Adam and Eve and instructed them to be fruitful and multiply. Sex then, originally was given as an agent for procreation, a method of bringing offspring into the world to populate it. Yet, in the doing, it also provides a catalyst to bring man and woman even closer in their relationship with one another. They actually become one, united in love.

"They were naked, the man and his wife, and were not ashamed." No one feels more vulnerable than when he is completely unclothed. Most people have at one time dreamed of being naked, with onlookers staring at them. I get an uneasy feeling just wearing one of those robes they give you at the doctor's office during an examination. I am afraid someone will sneak up behind me and peek at my backside. No one likes to have his or her bare body indiscriminately viewed. Yet, a husband and wife can feel perfectly relaxed and comfortable naked in the presence of one another. There is no reason for shame in a married couples' bedroom. Sex is not a dirty word. In its' proper context, it is one of the most beautiful things God has given mankind. That proper context is between a man and his wife.

When did Adam and Eve get married, you may ask? Of course, there was no wedding ceremony as we know it today, but God created woman to be a helpmeet for man, and fill the obligation as his wife. Together they became the first husband and wife, ordained by God. Ever since, mankind has instituted wedding ceremonies, recognizing that God is the instigator of marriage. In essentially every known culture in the world, from ancient times until today, the uniting of a man and woman in matrimony has been performed as a religious ceremony, sanctioned by a deity. From the tiny village in darkest Africa to the largest cathedral in Europe, the rites of marriage carry the same basic theme. God, or some other deity, is invoked to bless the couple, giving them peace, prosperity, happiness and healthy offspring. The ceremony may be short, lasting only a few minutes, or it may run for several days, but the end result is the same, to unite a man and a woman in wedlock.

In every civilization, from ancient Mesopotamia to twenty-first century Any Town, U.S.A., the expectations for the wedded couple have been identical, to stay together, rear a family and be a vital part in the community. Broken marriages not only devastate the husband and wife involved, but hurt children and tend to be detrimental to society as a whole. As alluded to earlier, in this country the divorce rate is approaching two-thirds of all marriages. Studies show the two major causes of breakups relate to finances and infidelity. For now, we will look at the latter.

Two of the Ten Commandments given by God to Moses relate to the indiscriminate use of sex, one specifically and one implied. Commandment number seven says, "You shall not commit adultery." It is specific, no questions asked, you just do not have sex outside of marriage and continue in God's grace. Webster defines adultery as, "voluntary sexual intercourse between a married man and someone other than his wife or between a married woman and someone other than her husband." That is not too difficult to understand, is it? God's rule simply put, states that you do not participate in sex with anyone other than your spouse. When a person commits adultery, they cause the other participant in the act to commit adultery also, whether they are married of not. Do you really wish to cause another person to sin and break God's commandments?

In the tenth commandment, the last one given, God says a person should not covet what another man has, including his wife. In other words, a person should not crave to own what another man owns. Realistically, there is only one reason a man would want to have another man's wife, and that is to have sex with her. God says we should not even think about sex with another man's wife. Jesus once said, "When a man looks upon a woman with lust, he has already committed adultery in his heart." This is reason enough to stay away from pornography and other types of sexually explicit material.

There are many instances recorded in the Bible where sex outside of marriage caused serious problems, not only for those committing the act, but also to their families, their descendents and even their nation. We will now look at two of the most well known.

Abraham is thought of as the one person most exemplifying faith in the entire Bible, and so he should be. He is the patriarchal father of three of the world's largest religions, Judaism, Islam and Christianity. Yet, this great man of faith had his lapses, and one of them has plagued the Israelites for four thousand years, even to today. God spoke to Abraham in Genesis 15:5, with a promise"

"Look now toward heaven, and tell the stars if you are able to number them; and so shall your seed be."

Abraham was assured that through his seed there would be more descendents than could be counted. In verse six, we see that Abraham believed God's promise.

When we get into Genesis chapter 16, however, we see Abraham's faith wavering. Sarah, his wife, is growing old and they still have no children. Has God forgotten his promise? Sarah suggests to Abraham that he go to bed with Hagar, her handmaid, in an attempt to conceive a son and heir. Rather than relying on the promise of God, verse two in chapter 16 tells us Abraham "hearkened to the voice of Sarah." With his wife's permission and persistent urging, he breaks his wedding vows and commits adultery with

Hagar. Hagar bore him a son, who they named Ishmael. Keep in mind in all of this, Hagar has no choice, she is a servant who must obey her masters.

Resentment towards Hagar enters the heart of Sarah, and when Sarah herself bares a son, Isaac, she demands that Ishmael and his mother be banished from the community and sent into the wilderness. Oftentimes, we tend to forget how cruel the patriarchs and matriarchs of the Bible were, on occasion. These men and women of God were a long way from being perfect, just as we are. Yet, God continued to bless them. Know that when you fail, God still loves, forgives and watches over you.

So Abraham follows the demands of his wife and, against his better judgment, exiles Hagar and Ishmael. Abraham abandoned Hagar, but God did not.

"The angel of God called to Hagar out of heaven, and said unto her, 'what ails you Hagar? Fear not; for God has heard the voice of the lad (Ishmael) where he is. Arise, lift up the lad, and hold him in your hand, for I will make him a great nation.'" Genesis 21:17,18

Banished by his father, Ishmael grew up in the wilderness with his mother, became a renown archer and married an Egyptian. Many years later, his descendent, Mohammed, established the Islamic religion, one of the largest of the World Religions. Muslims and Jews have a hatred for one another that has spanned the centuries, even though they are essentially cousins. Pick up any of today's newspapers and you can read about bombings, murders and military actions between Israelis and Palestinians or Arabs. Indeed, the entire world has felt the effects of their animosities. And all of this happened, because one man of great faith was unfaithful for a short period of time.

David was a mighty king, the greatest Israel has ever known. Though he was a man of God, he was also a warrior who had conquered nearly all of his enemies. He built Israel into a mighty and respected nation, feared by those around them. Maybe after all of his of his victories, he found too much time on his hands. In any case, one evening, as he was viewing his kingdom from a rooftop, his eyes beheld a beautiful woman taking a bath in a courtyard below him. David was a married man; he had no business looking. Of course, one cannot help a quick glance, that's what temptation is. Resisting temptation is turning away and not taking a second glance. David didn't bother to resist, however, in fact, he stared, and as he stared, he fantasized about making love to this beautiful woman whom he did not know. Sin always begins in the mind first, then it is acted upon.

Little is revealed concerning the actual encounter between David and Bathsheba. The entire tryst is covered quite quickly in two verses, II Samuel 11:3,4. There we read that David sent messengers to Bathsheba's home to bring her to him, where he lay with her, and then she returned to her house. Doesn't sound like either a very romantic or dramatic encounter when you read it, does it? Surely, there had to have been more.

I envision David slipping back into his palace bedroom, after returning from his rooftop walk. The thought of the lovely form he had just been ogling lingered in his mind.

"What a beautiful, voluptuous body, with its' sensuous curves and crevices," the image tantalized his thoughts. He could still see the long black hair, the hazel eyes and the almond skin, as the bath waters flowed over it. The mighty king found he could stand it no longer. He sent messengers to find out who she was.

The answer quickly came back. Her name was Bathsheba and she was married to Uriah, a captain in David's army. Off limits, then, she belonged to another, and adultery was punishable by death. Power can do strange things to people and, after all, David was king, he had ultimate power, or so he thought. He sent his messengers to Bathsheba's home with instructions to bring her to him.

Can you imagine how she must have felt, being escorted into the palace to stand before the king? Had she unknowingly committed some transgression? Had her husband been killed in action? What possibly could King David want with her? So she stands before the throne, visibly nervous, wondering what is going to happen to her. With desire building inside him, David stares at her beauty once again, sensing her vulnerability. Then he motions for her to approach the throne, where he explains why he has asked her to come. Most assuredly, she is shocked. Can this actually be happening, and dare she refuse? She is only one minor subject in this vast kingdom, the man before her is all-powerful. With one wave of his hand, he could have her slain. She doesn't take the chance. She concedes to the wishes of the monarch.

David can hardly wait; he rushes Bathsheba into his bedroom, lust filling his every fiber. In a matter of minutes, he is spent. It's all over. The end of verse four simply says, she returned to her house. The sinful act has been consummated. What's the big deal? David, the king, is satisfied and everyone should be happy.

Bathsheba is not happy, a man that should have been her protector, the king, has humiliated her and caused her to be unfaithful to the man she loves. On top of that, she becomes pregnant, which leads to David sinking deeper into the clutches of sin by having her husband murdered. One sin piles up upon another until, finally, the prophet Nathan reveals David for the blasphemer he has become. The son of David and Bathsheba's union dies because of David's adultery, and later his family is pulled apart by dissentions and plots. Two generations later the very kingdom is split in to because of the king's despicable act. No one, prophet or king, is so powerful that he can snub his nose at God's laws.

Now let's take a look at what the Bible says about sex in marriage. First of all, sex was made and ordained by God. In Genesis 1:28, God tells Adam and Eve to be fruitful and multiply. Chapter 2:24 says, "a man shall leave his father and his mother, and cleave unto his wife, and they shall be one flesh." Take a look at Genesis 1:31. "God saw every thing that he had made, and behold, it was *very* good." That included sex. This act we call sex has been the downfall of many a person, but it is also the most wonderful thing ever given to man and woman. God created it, ordained it, and made it Holy. Sex is not something to be joked about, ridiculed or misused.

A friend of mine from South Carolina and I were talking one day and the subject of lust came up. Sorry, ladies, but we men at times do discuss items other than sports and cars. My friend made the statement that a man should never have lust in his heart for a woman. I took exception to that view. Webster defines lust thusly,

"Pleasure, delight, a personal inclination, an intense longing or graving, usually connected to sexual desire. Eagerness, enthusiasm."

Isn't this the way a man should feel about his wife? Shouldn't a husband be eager and enthusiastic about the very thought of making love to his wife? I believe having a desire and graving for your wife is good and commendable. My friend never changed his point of view, but thank goodness, neither did I.

I agree that sex originally was made for procreation, a method to replenish the earth. Should it be used for pleasure? Does the Bible give us license for the marital bed to be a place of entertainment or enjoyment? I would direct you to read "Song of Solomon" sometime. It is a graphic detail of love between a man and his wife.

Proverbs 5:18,19 reads, *"Let thy fountain be blessed: and rejoice with the wife of thy youth. Let her be as the loving hind and pleasant roe; let her breasts satisfy thee at all times; and be thou ravished always with her love."*

Doesn't sound very much like an act of torture, does it? Rejoice with the wife of your youth. Be happy together. Enjoy one another's company, not just in youth, but as you grow old together. Let her satisfy you at all times, in your twenties and in your seventies. Be ravished with her love. Let her enfold you and excite you. Perhaps you can understand now why I believe a man should lust after his wife.

Husbands, never be afraid to show a little affection to your wife. Touch her hair, or brush her arm as you pass her chair. Tell her something flattering every day. Let her know you still desire her, and never forget to say, "I love you" often. My father left us when I was very young, but I was lucky to have a man in the neighborhood that would take me on vacation with his family, because his son and I were very close. One summer, we were staying in a cabin on the Shenandoah River in western Virginia. The wife was laboring over the stove cooking pancakes one morning, while my friend, his brother and I sat around a huge oaken table. Her husband came up behind her and wrapped an arm around her waist. He slipped his other hand under her dress and ran it up her thigh. Immediately, she screamed, "Honey, not in front of the kids."

I was too young to know the full ramifications of his act at the time, but I sensed it had been done in love. I also noticed how aglow her face was, even though she pretended to be angry with her husband. A small pat in the right places every once in a while can do wonders for a marital relationship.

The sexual relationship between a man and his wife is a private affair. No one else, not even mothers-in-law, need to know what goes on between a couple in their marital bed. I am totally confused when I read studies describing how many times a week, or month, certain couples, usually separated by age groups, have sex and what types of sex they participate in. Many of these surveys go into intricate detail. To make matters worst, our tax money finances many of these studies. Why on earth would anyone want to discuss so private a matter with perfect strangers? On the other hand, why would anyone care to know what other couples are doing? If I am ever asked to answer such a survey, my reply will be, "Enough to keep me happy." That's all they need to know.

There is nothing wrong then with having pleasure and enjoyment in the sex act. Sex is more than procreating and providing enjoyment, however. It is a responsibility. Listen to the words of I Corinthians 7:3-5:

"Let the husband render unto the wife due benevolence: and likewise also the wife unto the husband. The wife hath not power of her own body, but the husband: and likewise the husband hath not power of his own body, but the wife. Defraud ye not one the other, except it be with consent for a time, that ye may give yourselves to fasting and prayer; and come together again."

Many jokes have been told about women who have a headache at just the right, or wrong, depending on your perspective, time.

Unfortunately, this scenario plays out much more often than it should, and it is not always the wife who has the headache. The scripture states emphatically that the husband and the wife render due benevolence to one another. When a couple wed, they become one flesh; their bodies no longer belong to themselves, but to their spouses. We are not talking here about when a spouse is actually sick or incapacitated; we are talking about one spouse deliberately denying another spouse the sexual fulfillment that is rightfully his or hers.

I can anticipate someone reading this and saying, "Well, sometimes I just don't feel like it." That is all well and good, but it is hardly an excuse. I didn't feel like going to work some days, but I got up and went anyway, because I had an obligation to my employer. You have an obligation and a responsibility to your spouse. Go back and read that verse again. Doesn't it say, "Defraud you not one another?" I did not make the rules. God did. I am only a messenger, hoping to enlighten the reader.

There are married couples that, due to various reasons, including those that are health related, no longer participate in sex. That is certainly their decision to make, as long as both agree. Remember that sexual union is only one facet of a marital relationship. A friend at church was relating to me what he considered to be a problem with a married couple we both know. This couple has been married for quite a few years, and has two teenage children. According to my friend, the couple had not slept together for over ten years, and in his opinion, they should go on and get a divorce.

First of all, I don't need to know about this couple's marital affairs, unless one of them wishes to confide in me. It is none of my business, and quite frankly, it is none of the friend's business either.

The point my friend is missing, however, is that marriage is much, much more than having sex. It is a commitment under God not to be broken. A man and a woman can love one another deeply, living together in a harmonious environment, without practicing sex. Indeed, especially in later years, some couples are seeking only companionship and a secure home life.

7

FAMILY FINANCES

"For the love of money is the root of all evil: which while some coveted after, they have erred from the faith, and pierced themselves through with many sorrows." I Timothy 6:10

"What a strange scripture verse to begin this chapter with?" you may be asking. Before you criticize me for its' inappropriateness, read on to see my rationale for using it. In Chapter Six, I mentioned that finances, along with infidelity, were the two major causes of marital breakups. Those breakups occur in every stratum of society, regardless of family income. Millionaires, living in mansions on estates, with rolling acreage are divorcing, along with couples barely meeting the poverty level, and residing in a one-bedroom apartment. So, it is obviously not a matter of having a lot of money or not that is causing the problem, it is how husbands and wives are viewing the use of the money they do have.

In Genesis, we saw that God placed Adam in the Garden of Eden to tend and keep it. We no longer live in the garden, but God has provided us with material gifts, including money, and expects us to take care of it. How we use and spend our money paints a vivid picture of who we are, and what we really care about. If you want to learn what a person enjoys, and his attitude toward life, read the stubs in his checkbook. A golfer will have stubs made out to his country club for annual dues and weekly green fees, along with other stubs for golf shoes, clubs and miscellaneous golf related equipment. Theatergoers will show checks written for Broadway plays and, possibly airline tickets to New York. Maybe there will be checks made out for hotels and restaurants in the Big Apple. Someone who loves his local church will have stubs for weekly or monthly tithes, and an occasional special offering. A person will put his money where his heart is; this is an inevitable fact of life.

When a man and woman wed, they become one flesh, united in a lifetime partnership. What belongs to one belongs to the other, right? That is what the preacher said. Yet, when the husband realizes that someone other that himself has access to his bank account, strange things start to happen. Oh, he knows she needs to buy groceries, pay doctor's bills and keep herself looking nice, but just how far does she have to go? He has plenty of money in the account, but he wasn't aware she had so many magazine subscriptions, or just how much sewing machines and materials cost. She is spending way too much of his money, and he lets her know it. He is going to tighten the purse strings. Feelings are hurt as the husband and wife argue over finances.

A wife may also work, spending eight hours a day on the job to help support their income. The husband wants a new car and together they determine what they can afford. One day, he drives home in a Cadillac Deville, excited about his purchase and wanting to show off all the options he bought. The wife hits the ceiling, knowing there is no way they can pay for that car. Feelings are again hurt.

In the first case, the husband is possessive of the finances in the family. He looks on the bank account as his money. Isn't he so generous to be letting her use some of it? In the second case, the man is not even worried about money; only what it can buy him. What harm can a little debt do?

It is not money itself that causes distress, but the attitude an individual has towards it. Our scripture says, "The love of money is the root of all evil." We could easily expand this to include the love of material possessions, which takes money to purchase. A person can get so wrapped up in owning things; he or she can bring a marriage to the precipice of disaster.

Studies made in 2000 showed that thirty-seven percent of Americans were considered so deep in debt, they were a paycheck away from bankruptcy. Bankruptcies were at an all time high for individuals. Remember, this was before the downturn in the U.S. economy. Figures would probably be even worst, should a study be taken today. Being in debt causes emotional stress in a family that can destroy even a strong relationship.

So what are God's rules when it comes to money? I think there are three. You may want to add some others, but these will do quite nicely:

1. Manage it properly

2. Tithe

3. Be a partnership

Whatever you possess, God has given it to you. "Know you not that all good things come from God?" Whether you are rich or barely getting by, your resources should be handled in a judicious manner.

In Matthew 25:14-30, Jesus tells a story about three men who were given various amounts of talents, an amount of money in that day. One man was given ten talents, one, five talents and the last man, one talent. While their master was away, the first two men doubled their talents by proper investment. The third, however, buried his talent in the ground and gained nothing. When the master returned, he rewarded the first two equally, but he took the one talent away from the third man. The lesson here is to use what we have been given wisely.

Every husband and wife should develop a workable and realistic budget that includes all normal expenses, and allows some flexibility for emergencies. Don't forget to show monies for entertainment and vacations. These are not rewards, but are important items that provide relaxation and togetherness. Assign responsibilities for keeping up with each item. Perhaps the wife could handle the groceries and routine monthly bill paying and the husband is responsible for big money items and setting aside money for vacation.

Keep track of spending, savings and other investments. Try to stay within your budget. Avoid impulse buying and spending excessively to impress friends and family. This is especially true when it comes to buying gifts. If you can't afford it, don't do it. Most important of all, use credit cards sparingly, and when you do, pay them off totally each month.

Hopefully, your budget will show a tithe to your local place of worship. Tithing is a financial act of faith; concrete evidence that you believe in God's promises. It is merely giving back to God ten percent of what he has already given you. The idea of the tithe first appears in the Bible in Genesis, Chapter 14. Abram has had a successful campaign against the kings of Sodom and Gomorrah, bringing back the goods that the kings had possessed. He comes to the high priest, Melchizedek, to be blessed. In verses 19 and 20, we read:

And he blessed him, and said, "Blessed be Abram of the most high God, possessor of heaven and earth; and blessed be the most high God, which has delivered thine enemies into thy hand," And he (Abram) gave him (Melchizedek) tithes of all of it.

Leviticus 27:30 states, "And all the tithe of the land, whether of the seed of the land, or the fruit of the tree, is the Lord's; it is holy unto the Lord." The Israelites believed, and still do, that the tithe must be given to God before they could use any portion of the rest. That is the test of faith, to believe God will give you the ability to survive on the remaining ninety percent. To wait until your next pay period and then give ten percent to your church is not tithing. It is only giving God what is left.

Beginning to tithe is difficult, but it is an excellent way to test your faith. The idea of tithing did not come easy to me. When I was a boy, my mother taught me to tithe. I remember her giving me nickels and dimes to put in the offering, and explaining to me how God's work was carried out. Later, I would set aside this change myself, when I was given cash for birthdays or Christmas, or earned a little on my own. At that time, there was not a lot of money involved. I grew up, got married and began making more, but I also had more things to spend it on, rent, a car, the groceries. You know the routine. So I stopped tithing.

My wife would often bring up the fact that we should be tithing and I always had my excuses ready.

"Remember, we are saving for a down payment on a home," I would say, or "We need new tires." I was never without reasons why we could not afford to tithe. After all, we were barely getting by, as it was. How could we make it on ten percent less?

My company transferred me to Baton Rouge, Louisiana, giving me a twenty percent increase in salary. Immediately, Kay started in again. "It's time we began tithing," she said. Admittedly, I had more than I had ever expected, but now we lived in a house costing twice as much as the one we left. We also now had two children to provide for, plus we needed a second car. There was simply no way I could see tithing and now, a tenth would be even more each month.

"No way, Kay," I reiterated, as I had many times in the past. "Maybe later, we can try it."

We joined a church and I immediately began working with young people, teens through college. The second year there, the preacher and chairman of deacons, approached me, wanting to know if I would accept a nomination for the office of deacon. I told them I would consider it and let them know later. For several days, I wrestled with the idea. First of all, I wasn't sure I was spiritual enough, but mainly, I felt to be a deacon, a man must tithe. I declined the nomination.

"Why don't you just begin tithing?" my wife asked.

"It's not that easy," I responded. "I really don't think we can afford it."

"I don't think we can afford not to, if we are going to grow spiritually, we need to step out on faith."

I made a point of talking to Gerald Chancellor, our pastor, about my feelings. He made me a proposition.

"Try tithing for one year. If you find you really miss the money, then stop. I believe you will never notice the difference. If you try and I'm wrong, I promise never to preach another sermon on tith-ing."

On my next payday, I sat down to write a check to the church. It was all I could do to make the pen move on the paper, but I finally got it written. That night, I lie awake wondering if I had made the right decision. At least, Kay was pleased.

"Just wait until she needs money for something," I thought to myself.

The second month was a little easier, as was the third, and every month after that. All of our bills were getting paid. We ate well. We even went out once in a while. There did not seem to be any change in our standard of living. The year passed, and I can truly say, I never missed a penny of the money I gave to the church. A couple of things did change, however. Earlier, I said that a person would spend his money on the things that interest him. There is a corollary to that. When a person spends his money on something, he takes more interest in it. I became more interested in how the church was run; I attended business meetings and voted on how church finances were used. The greatest change, however, was my attitude toward finances and the strengthening of my faith to rely on God. Hebrews 13:5 reads, "Keep your lives free from the love of money and be content with what you have."

The third rule I postulated was, "Be a partnership." It is a strange fact of life that it is easier to give another person ones' body, heart and soul, than it is to allow that person to have access to ones' money. It is as if we say to our spouse, "Honey, I love you deeply, you mean all the world to me and I just couldn't go on in life with-out you, but keep your hands away from my checkbook."

How utterly ridiculous! When a husband and wife become one flesh, their bank accounts become one asset. The only proper way to handle that asset is jointly as partners. In a partnership, everything that is done is for the mutual benefit of both parties. Any major decision regarding finances must be discussed by the partnership. As mentioned earlier, there is nothing at all wrong with one or the other handling the finances, as long as that partner realizes those finances belong to both parties. If a couple is to be one in every other phase of their marital relationship, doesn't it make sense that they are one in their financial affairs also?

Many couples in today's society have taken up the practice of having separate checking accounts. It is not for me to judge whether this is a good practice or not, but I can see a real danger in each spouse considering that his or her account is their money. The U.S. government even encourages the practice by the method IRAs are set up. Rather than allow joint accounts for a couple, each spouse is allowed a certain amount per annum to set aside in personal IRA savings accounts.

It is important, however, that each spouse have some cash that they can spend as they wish on incidentals, call it an allowance, spending money, or what have you. One spouse should not have to go to the one handling the finances and ask for money each time they need something. This practice can become demeaning for the spouse that has to always be asking.

I learned this lesson early in my marriage. My wife did not work and I handled all of our finances. Each week, I gave her money for groceries and that was basically it. Whenever she wanted cash for spending, she would come to me and ask for it. I never refused to give her what she asked for, but that wasn't the point. The point was she had to ask; she depended on me for every cent. At that time, I was young and ignorant. At least, now I am not so young and I have acquired a little knowledge about human nature.

When she had enough, she let me know it as only a wife can. Of course, I was shocked; I thought the system was working fine. Through tears, she explained to me how it felt to always have to come to me for money. We developed a different system. We set aside money in a drawer for our use at any time we needed something personal. In reality, I have only taken money from the drawer several times in over forty years. It worked. She was happy and at the end of almost every pay period the drawer was empty. She has since begun working, but money is still placed in a drawer every pay period. Oddly, even though she now has money of her own to spend, the drawer still is empty at the end of the month.

To be partners is a matter of building trust. A husband trusts his wife to be faithful to the marriage vows; he must trust her to be faithful with the family finances. All the money in the world will not bring about a happy marriage. More important is the attitude a couple has towards the money they do possess, working together as partners under the leadership of God.

8

RAISING A FAMILY

"And Adam knew Eve, his wife; and she conceived, and bare Cain, and said, 'I have gotten a man from the Lord.' And she again bare his brother, Abel. And Abel was a keeper of sheep, but Cain was a tiller of the ground."

The newlyweds are getting along fantastically, how could they be happier? They move into a nice one-bedroom apartment, overlooking a beautiful park with a gorgeous view. Both of their jobs begin to really take off; there is extra money for minor luxuries, and some even left over to open a savings account. They are learning one another's idiosyncrasies and really adapting to the marital lifestyle, a perfect union of husband and wife, stepping out into the "happy ever after" phase of life. Then it happens. The wife becomes pregnant.

Suddenly, everything has changed. There is a new sense of responsibility. Money will be tighter; those minor luxuries may have to be put off to a later date. The one-bedroom apartment may be too small. The wife, now becoming a mother, may choose to stay home to raise her son or daughter, leaving them with only one income. They are going to have a baby, and that is the one thing that should make them happier as a couple.

Remember God's instruction to Adam and Eve? "Be fruitful and multiply." What is happening here is a God ordained occurrence, it is what marriage and, indeed, life is all about. This is why in all cultures, the coming together of a man and a woman in matrimony is honored and blessed. Likewise, when a child is born, it is a cause of celebration for the entire community. A family has begun.

Someone once said, "If you want to show love to your children, love their mother." A corollary to that statement is, "If you want to show love to your wife, love her children." Nothing gives a woman more pleasure, than seeing her husband caring for and playing with her offspring. As a young father, it felt natural for me to come home from work and frolic with my son and daughter. I enjoyed rolling on the floor with them, throwing them in the air, and all the many things fathers do. I must admit, I never paid much attention to my wife's reaction at the time; after all, I was having too much fun playing with the two munchkins I loved. I now know that those times that gave me so much pleasure also provided pleasure for my wife.

I observe my daughter's reaction now, when she watches her husband play with their three boys. She totally beams at the sight of them having such a good time together. She even enjoys when grandma and grandpa give the boys attention. Take the time to let the love for your children show, it will go a long way to maintaining a happy wife.

Unfortunately, playing with children when they are young may be the easiest part of raising them, bringing them to adulthood is fraught with many problems. Children must be taught discipline and understanding, and it is the responsibility of the husband to take the lead in this training.

Proverbs 22:6 says, *"Train up a child in the way he should go: and when he is old, he will not depart from it."* The admonition in this passage is geared toward the religious training of the child, but also could include morals, ethics and building integrity. Our writer in Proverbs is stating that if the child is trained correctly, even though for a time he may depart from that training, in later life he will return to it. This should be a reassuring scripture for those of you that have teenagers.

Remember, to properly train someone, you must show him what is to be learned, not merely tell him how to do it. Try telling a small child how to tie his shoestrings, explaining the way the cord loops around and pulls together. He will not understand, and quickly become frustrated. I am not quite sure I would understand the procedure, just hearing the method. If you take the string, however, and allow the child to watch as you begin to tie it together, he will watch and learn. Soon, he will take the strings and begin trying himself, and before you know, he has perfected the tie. Most of what an individual learns is from what he sees and does, not from what he hears.

The older a child becomes, the more important this principle holds. Telling a daughter she should pray and read her Bible will have no effect, unless she sees you in communication with God. It will simply not seem important to her, if she doesn't see you setting an example for her. Likewise, you can't train a child not to lie, steal or cheat, if at the same time you do those very things. Let your children see you pray and read the Bible. Let them observe you are a man of your word. How can you explain the dangers of smoking when you yourself light up? The real training you give your son or daughter is in your example.

Paul, in Ephesians 6:4 states, *"Fathers, provoke not your children to wrath: but bring them up in the nurture and admonition of the Lord."* Again, we see the father is challenged to provide religious education for his children. Many fathers today take a back seat, and allow the kids to learn about God at Sunday school and church or let the mother provide this phase of their education. What a shame. It is important to take your children to Sunday school and church, but what they hear there should be supplementing what you are already teaching them. Begin at an early age to read Bible stories to your children and teach them to pray. Believe me, the experience will be just as rewarding for you as it is for your children.

There are some practical aspects of raising children a husband and wife need to agree on. One is discipline, how and when should it be applied and who does it? To be effective, especially with younger children, discipline must be administered fairly, consistently and swiftly. How a couple chooses to discipline is up to them. Whether to spank or give some other type of punishment depends on the nature and age of the child involved. Being from the old school, I believe in administering the flat part of the hand to the backside of the child, but I realize in modern society this may be considered child abuse. Nevertheless, it is a proven method of discipline that has worked for ages.

Spanking doesn't always work, however. My son did not respond to spankings, but we found that taking away his right to view TV worked wonders. Each child is an individual and will respond differently. The married couple needs to learn what works best with each of their children, and then administer that discipline consistently. Do not allow a child to do something one day without punishment, and then punish him or her the next day for the same violation.

They will be receiving mixed signals and won't know what they are supposed to do.

My wife had a practice of sometimes, after one of the children had misbehaved, telling them to "Wait until your father gets home." I never felt this was fair, either to me or to the child in question. Coming home from work, the last thing I wanted to do was to punish a child for something I had not seen occur. My thoughts were of getting down on the floor to play, or taking them to the pool beside our house. Administering a spanking always seemed to ruin the moment. My son or daughter, on the other hand, had to wait all day worrying about the spanking he or she knew they were going to get when I got home. Since grown, they both told me that the waiting was even worst than the spanking itself. The parent who observes misbehavior in their child should administer discipline as quickly as possible, letting the child know why they are being disciplined.

Some child psychologists today promote the idea that children do not require discipline. They adhere to a theory that rewarding children is the best way of training them. To some extent, I agree with giving a child a reward for something well done as a method of training. One good example would be when "potty" training. If the child manages to go properly, a cookie or other reward is in order. However, when a child puts itself in danger or deliberately disobeys, discipline is in order. How do you reward a small child for not sticking her finger in an electric outlet? When that finger heads toward that outlet, a quick slap of the hand indicates to the child that that is something that should not be done. Talking back to parents and other acts of misbehavior cannot be condoned, if a couple wants their child to grow into a responsible adult.

Lack of discipline in teenagers usually equates to a lack of discipline in the early stages of childhood. There would be fewer young people on drugs, experiencing unwed pregnancies and committing teenage crime, if parents began early in life to teach them morals, values and respect for others. This is a God given responsibility.

The showing of favoritism has been detrimental to many a family. Even Godly families in the Bible had a problem with this. Isaac and Rebekah are the classic example of how a family can be split. Isaac loved Esau because he was manly and a huntsman. Rebekah favored Jacob, who was fair-skinned and handsome. Isaac wished to confer the family blessing upon Esau, but Rebekah conspired with Jacob to have him receive the blessing. So what was the result? Jacob was forced to leave his family and live apart from them in a foreign land for many years. He lived in fear of his brother Esau. Eventually, the brothers were reunited, but think of all Jacob missed by not living at home, and all because of his mother's favoritism.

Never play favorites with your children. Each one is different. Some may give you more sorrow than others, but you owe the same amount of love and attention to each one. They will more than likely think the others get more attention anyway, but don't allow it to be real. My daughter still believes my wife and I let her brother get away with more than she was allowed. This may in some way be true, but it was because she was the oldest and a girl; it had nothing to do with favoritism.

There is no thing more important in raising children, than spending time with them, individually and as a family. About twenty years ago, a recording entitled, "Cat's in the Cradle" was on the top ten list. The song described how a father could not find the time to play with his young son. Yet, the boy wanted to grow up to be just like his dad. As the lad grew, the father was occupied with other things, what he considered the important things in life. When the son was grown, the father called, wanting to build a relationship, but, unfortunately, the son had grown go be just like him. What a wasted opportunity.

Many times, the causes we neglect our children for are good. While I was Youth Director at our church in Baton Rouge, I found myself spending most of my weekends, plus some nights with the youth of the church. Youth ministry is important. At the time, I was President of the Baton Rouge Credit Union Chapter, plus I had a full time job. These endeavors take time. One night, as I was about to go out the door, my daughter, who was about four at the time, came up to me. She pulled on my pants leg, looked up with her turquoise eyes, and said, "Daddy, when are you going to spend a night with me?"

A knife turning in my heart could have not hurt any more. What was I doing with my life? Why hadn't I seen that I was neglecting the most precious things I possessed, my children? I picked her up, held her close and said, "Tonight, honey, tonight." I called a friend from church and asked him to cover for me because something had come up. Then, my daughter and I went to McDonald's for a milk shake.

Ever since my daughter was three, I have taken her out to eat on her birthday, just the two of us. When my son reached three, I began the same celebration with him. They get to select the restaurant. In the early days, it was almost always McDonald's, but as they grew, the restaurants became more and more expensive. My daughter is now thirty-six and we still continue the practice, even though she has three children of her own.

My wife and I always managed to schedule a week's vacation each year for the family, even though there was some years we could barely afford it. With the children's help, we would select a city to visit, one that had a major league baseball park, a zoo and an amusement park nearby. Nothing can replace the memories of driving throughout these United States with my wife and children. Another book could be written just from those experiences.

Spend time with each child separately and spend time together as a family. Attend their sporting and extracurricular activities and be active in their school life. We hear the expression today, "quality time". Believe me, any time spent in an activity with your children will be quality time.

9

GROWING TOGETHER

"Be careful that you do not forget the Lord your God, failing to observe his commands, his laws and his decrees that I am giving you this day."
Deuteronomy 8:11

It is quite easy to become "one flesh" physically; it is quite another thing to become "one flesh" spiritually. Much emphasis is placed on the honeymoon, a time when the new bride and groom can spend time alone to begin to know each other. Thousands of dollars are expended, just to get the proper setting, the right environment, for that first night alone together. Yet, when the honeymoon is over, what have they really learned about one another. Yes, they have experienced the physical union that finalizes the wedding vows. They have shared and enjoyed the excitement of some tropical paradise or resort area, maybe even cruised on a luxurious ocean liner, but what knowledge have they acquired about the real person they will be expected to live with for the rest of their lives?

Honeymoons take place in controlled environments, usually in a lavish hotel or, possibly, a villa by the seashore. Entertainment and exquisite meals abound on every side. Waiters and bellhops cater to the couple's every need. They may dance, lie on a beach or attend a lavish dinner party. Everyone around them is happy and life is good. So for the first few days of marriage, the couple sees one another in this extravagant setting. Now, I believe everyone who can afford it should definitely go on a honeymoon when they become married, but a honeymoon is not conducive for a couple to really get to know each other as they truly are. That begins when the couple wakes up one morning living together in the real world.

Living in the same house or apartment with another individual is never easy. After the wedding celebration and honeymoon is over, a husband and his new wife have a tremendous amount of adjusting to do, just to survive the everyday situations of life. Just sleeping together may be difficult. Each has more than likely been sleeping alone, in a room filled with only their belongings. Does one snore or move around all night in bed? Lack of sleep can test any relationship.

Even sharing a bathroom can present a variety of problems. Who showers first? Does the wife wait for her husband to shave or does he wait for her to do her hair? Some people want complete privacy when in the bathroom, others may be used to barging in at any time. Will a wife hanging her panty hose to dry in the shower irritate the husband? This is just an inkling of the thousands of little intrusions of space a man and his wife must face each and every day they live together.

Did God know all this when he created Eve? Of course He did, and He knew she still would be the greatest enjoyment in Adam's life, as any good wife is to her husband. God also is aware that a man and his wife will do one of two things, they will grow closer together or they will drift apart, both spiritually and physically. That's why He laid down His commands, laws and decrees, to help us draw closer. As a husband and wife grow closer to God individually, they will grow closer to one another as a couple. That is why it is important to establish healthy spiritual practices in the home early in a marriage relationship.

Church records inform us that the majority of young people cease attending church services soon after they are married. This is true for all religions, in both eastern and western cultures. No one is really sure why this happens. Perhaps, the young couples just want to spend more time together and need time to adjust to their new place in society as a married couple. Fortunately, usually when children arrive on the scene, these couples return to their base of faith.

I remember this happening in my own life soon after I was married, and I also remember that some of the worst sins I ever committed occurred during the time I was away from the church. The scripture text for this chapter says, "Be careful that you forget not the Lord, your God." It is much easier to forget God when you are not attending church regularly. Slipping away from God is a gradual process; you don't even realize it is happening to you. Luckily, I had a forgiving wife and a God that forgives all things. Just a point, God never slips away from us, we slip away from Him.

To grow spiritually, a young couple should worship together. Even when Christians marry, they may come from very diverse religious backgrounds. There are major differences between Episcopal and Pentecostal Holiness services. One spouse could be bored to death in an Episcopal setting, while the other might be scared out of his or her wits in a Pentecostal meeting. Fortunately, today there are a multitude of Christian denominations and affiliations that run the gamut between the two. A young married couple should visit around, until they find a fellowship that can satisfy both of their needs. It may mean that both will have to give somewhat on non-important issues they have practiced most of their lives.

Different churches and denominations have varying beliefs and creeds, although they all may be Christian. Many congregations within the same denomination do not agree on all issues. Some may baptize by sprinkling water on a person's head, while another group submerges their prospective members. Many mainline churches today have women deacons while others think this practice is horrid and unbiblical. These beliefs must be weighed against the beliefs of the couple to determine whether they can live with them or not. A word of caution here, there are many church groups that operate on the fringe of Christianity, but do not preach the entire gospel. Make sure whatever assembly you join preaches the God of the Old Testament, and a Jesus Christ who is the Son of God, born of a virgin, who died on a cross for the sins of all mankind and was bodily resurrected, who is now sitting on the right hand of God and is coming again to claim His church. Anyone believing on Jesus as the Son of God can have eternal life. The rest is subject to interpretation, which is why we have so many denominations.

Once a church fellowship has been agreed upon, take an active part in the worship services of the congregation. Develop a habit of attendance on Sunday morning, and go in an attitude of worship. Join Sunday school or Bible study classes where you can learn more about God's word. Keep in fellowship with other Christian couples who can give you support in your daily walk.

Building a close relationship with God does not happen just by going to church, however. In fact, if the only time a young couple open their Bibles is on Sunday, in church, it will be very difficult for them to mature spiritually. As good and needful as church worship is, it cannot replace the personal worship of individuals and couples in the home.

To not forget God's commandments, laws and decrees, a person must keep them before him daily. That means daily reading of God's word, the Bible. As the spiritual leader of the home, a husband should set the example for his household. He should set aside a time for personal devotions, when he can spend a few minutes talking to God in prayer and listening to God by reading the scriptures.

How long should these devotions take? Length is not as important as consistency and attitude. Daily devotions should not become a chore, something that must be done, rather, they should be something looked forward to. Five minutes is enough time to thank God for his blessings, read from His word and pray for the days' activities. Of course, if you have more time, that is fine too. Some are able to spend hours in devotions, but the key is to be consistent.

When should a person do their daily devotions? Again, timing is not the crucial issue, but the execution. For me, I like to have my personal devotions in the morning right after breakfast. It is a good way for me to start the day. Others I know like their devotions at night just before bedtime, so they can thank God for what he has done for them during the day. Select a time that is convenient for you and stick to it.

I have been discussing the husband, but it is equally important for the wife to have a private time with God also. Along with personal devotions, it is a good idea to have a shared devotion between husband and wife. Many excellent devotion books have been written for couples with topics and scriptures given for each day of the year. One I recommend highly is, Quiet Times For Couples by H. Norman Wright. My wife and I are going through it for the third year.

"The family that prays together stays together." I have heard this quote for a long time, though I don't know who first expressed it. A study was actually run in the sixties that determined this statement to be true. Thousands of families were interviewed, and the study showed that in the homes where prayer was practiced, whether the family was Christian, Jewish, Hindu, Muslim or whatever, the chances of divorce were astoundingly smaller than in families that did not practice prayer. Just the act of praying together had a binding effect on these husbands, wives and their families. As a sidebar, these families also had fewer problems with their children, fewer runaways, fewer teenage pregnancies and a more congenial home life than non-praying families.

Prayer is talking to God, praising His name, thanking Him for blessings received and asking for future blessings. What a tremendous feeling to be able to pray with your spouse in a time of need or in a time of celebration.

Husbands and wives, worship together, develop personal and joint devotion times and pray as one. Each of you will grow closer to God spiritually and, in so doing, you will be drawn closer together in a love relationship that many in this world may never understand.

10

THE MARRIAGE KNOT

"And the two shall be one flesh: so then they are no more two, but one flesh. What therefore God has joined together, let no man put asunder."
Mark 10:8,9

If nothing else is remembered from this epistle, let this one significant fact remain embedded in the mind of the reader. Marriage is an institution conceived, ordained and sanctioned by God. It is God's desire that a man and a woman unite in Holy matrimony to become one flesh for an entire lifetime. It is His wish that the couple bears children and raise a family, in the admonition of His direction and teaching. No one, man or woman, in-laws or outsiders, has any right to attempt to separate this couple from one another or from the love of God.

God cares so much for the continuation of a marriage between a man and a woman that He has laid down rules, which, if followed, will tie a husband and wife in a knot that cannot be broken. Let's take a moment to review those rules.

Rule 1: Seek a husband or wife within your own faith. "Be not unequally yoked together with unbelievers." The early Hebrews entering the Promised Land, intermarried with pagan idol worshipers. To appease their new wives, they were drawn away from God and His teachings. God punished the nation because of this. God had selected the Hebrews to be a people set apart and dedicated to Him, marrying only within their own race.

Christians should seek out other Christians when dating and looking for a lifetime mate. Being of a like faith will help in marriage when problems and travails arise. But, God does not wish couples to divorce just because they are of different faiths. He still holds each and every marriage sacred and Holy, and to be honored.

Rule 2: Break the apron strings. "For this cause shall a man leave his father and mother, and cleave to his wife." The word "cleave" today means the exact opposite of the biblical definition as given in this verse. Webster defines "cleave" as "to separate or divide with a large knife". A meat cleaver may come to mind. However, the biblical term meant to "adhere, cling or stick". Have you ever used duct tape and had it stick together on you? It is nearly impossible to pull apart. That is how a man should adhere to his wife, so stuck together they are one unit. Of course, we can use the modern definition to cleave or cut that apron string.

When a person marries, their focus in life changes from being under the watch care of a mother and father, to providing the watch care for their spouse. One family is left to begin another. The former home must be given up to start the new. The scripture is very clear that a person must leave his father and mother to unite with his or her spouse. In-laws should not try to run a newly wedded couples lives; it is contrary to God's rule.

Rule 3: Wives, submit to your husbands. Most Eastern cultures instruct young girls in the art of submission. They are taught to honor and respect their husbands even before they know whom their husband will be. They learn to cater to every whim of the prospective husband, in some cases, they may even learn the art of sexual satisfaction. It is only in the so-called "Christianized" western culture that there is a problem with the idea of a wife submitting herself to her husband. Yet, the Bible is crystal clear on the matter. Under God's direction, wives are instructed to submit themselves to their husbands.

Submission does not mean a woman allows herself to be abused, downtrodden or depersonalized. By submitting, she voluntarily agrees to serve the needs of her husband and support him in every manner possible. Should you ever travel and visit in the home of a Japanese, Chinese or another Asian couples' home, you will be quick to see that the wife is an integral part of that household. The respect and love of the husband for his wife will be immediately obvious, even though she has been submitting to him since their wedding vows.

I have good friends living in Kuala Lumpur, Malaysia. They are Hindu and the wife has been taught submission to husband from her childhood. It did not take me long to realize that, even though she submits to his will in most matters, she ruled the household. She also owned and managed three Indian restaurants in the city. Submissive, yes; but hardly suppressed. I was also deeply impressed by the closeness of their marital relationship.

There is an attitude of love and respect involved in the ability to submit oneself to another. A wife who possesses that attitude toward her mate wrote the following poem:

> *I married a man I respect*
> *I have no need to bow and defer.*

I married a man I adore and admire,

> *I don't need to be handed a list entitled,*

> *"how to build his ego" or*

> *"the male need for admiration."*

Love, worship, loyalty, trust-these are inside me:

> *they motivate my actions.*

> *to reduce them to rules destroys my motivation.*

<u>*I choose to serve him, and enjoy him.*</u>

We choose to live together and grow together,

> *to stretch our capacities for love*

> *even when it hurts and looks like conflict.*

We choose to learn to know each other

> *as real people,*

> *as two unique individuals unlike any other two.*

Our marriage is a commitment of love:

> *to belong to each other*

> *to know and understand*

> *to care*

> *to share ourselves, our goals,*

> *interests, desires, needs.*

Out of that commitment the actions follow.

Love defines our behavior

> *and our ways of living together.*

And since we fail to meet not only the demands

> *of standards but also the simple requirements*

> *of love*

We are forced to believe in forgiveness…and
    grace.

What a wonderful expression of love and commitment, and the groundwork for total submission to her husband.

<u>Rule 4</u>: Husbands love your wives even as Christ loved the Church. Jesus Christ was perfect in every way, therefore His love for the Church was a perfect love. We husbands will never be able to love perfectly, because we are human, and humans make mistakes. Our goal, however, is to attempt to love as Christ did. In an earlier chapter, we discussed how God's love is to be shown to our wives, so I won't repeat myself. Suffice it to say, however, that in this world, a man's wife should be his reason for living, the total essence of life itself. Since I used a poem by a wife about her husband, it is only fitting I use a poem written by a husband about his wife. As you read, try to sense the deep love this husband has for his wife. He calls the poem, "The Nature of Love and Time."

A rare delicacy touches her soft cheek;
    she's no common girl.
There is a gentle elegance in her step,
    that charming elegance that loses not warmth.
I often quietly observe her.
Charm is not alone in clothes of sophistication;
    it seems to crown the simple things…
    a look, a touch, a smile
    the conveyance of beauty through being.
The tragedy of our love is time…

it takes time to capture the reality of
delicacy and elegant charm.
Yet...
    we may struggle with time or embrace him.
    He may be our guard at the prison gate
    or our liberator into each other.
As the hours seldom come to quietly observe
    you—my love
    I shall liberate the moments and drink
    of your touch, your smile, your look...
And consider great wealth those hours—
    even (God grant) days when,
    alone at last,
    we shall be enfolded by the warmth
    and beauty of our love.

What more could I add?

Rule 5: Be faithful to your spouse. Do not commit adultery. Of all God's rules relating to marriage, this is the most explicit, specific and easy to understand. Adultery is having sexual relations with someone other than your spouse. According to statistical reports, over eighty percent of men and nearly sixty percent of women have been unfaithful to their spouses at least once over the course of their marriage. Infidelity is the number one reason given for divorce in the United States, making sexual temptation by far the largest threat to destroying marriages. Many well-known preachers and other devout men of God have succumbed to the desires of the flesh by briefly letting down their guard.

Rule 6: Be financially responsible. Problems with money are the other major cause of divorce. Don't gamble away family resources or take on excessive debt. Learn to trust God to provide your needs by instituting the practice of tithing. Remember, the Bible tells us that the love of money is the root of all evil. Use your earthly resources wisely, but put your faith in a heavenly father.

Rule 7: Bring up your children in the knowledge and admonition of God. Teach them to pray, and set a Godly example in the home. Instruct in proper morals and ethics and display these in your daily life. Show love to your spouse before your children, so they may develop a sense of security and warmth. Discipline fairly and consistently, and never exhibit favoritism. There may be times when your children will rebel, but remember God's promise, "Train up a child in the way he should go, and when he is old, he will not depart from it."

Rule 8: Worship and pray together. The first four of the Ten Commandments relate to a person's relationship to God. The psalms proclaim how we should praise and honor the name of God. As a married couple, you are now one flesh, and should jointly give praise to God for all he has done and provided to you. Pray earnestly for one another, and with each other, that God will direct you in your everyday life. Believe that God wants you to have a successful marriage; remembering that He created the family long before He created the church, and God gave His only Son for the church.

What has been established in this epistle? There are eight simple rules God has given us, which, if followed, will guarantee a long and happy marriage, barring an early unfortunate death to sickness or accident. Many more details could be gleaned from the scriptures concerning the marital relationship, but these eight are the basics. Every divorce that has occurred can be traced to either one or both spouses breaking one or more of these rules. You may be thinking, "Well, that is a very general statement to make," but I challenge you to consider the facts in each case and prove me wrong.

In every situation, you will find that either one spouse has been untrue to the other, causing hurt and resentment, or a wife doesn't feel the need to be submissive to her husband, or a husband doesn't love the wife in the proper biblical context. Maybe, the couple has drifted away from fellowship with God, and, in so doing, has drifted away from each other. Perhaps, a wife is tied to her parental apron strings, and will not give her husband the support and respect he deserves. Each and every case will reflect the breaking of at least one of God's rules.

So, if you find you and your spouse drifting apart, what should you do? Vince Lombardi, after the Green Bay Packers had had a particular bad game, said to the team in the locker room, "Gentlemen, let's go back to the basics." Then, he held up a football and explained how it was supposed to be used. The same advice is applicable when a married couple is having a particular hard time. Go back to the basics. Look at God's rules and determine where you and your spouse are failing. Then get back on track doing the things God wants you to do as a couple.

Husbands and wives are human, and humans make mistakes. The great patriarchs of the Bible made serious blunders with their family affairs, men like Abraham, Isaac, Jacob and David. If these great men of God made serious errors in judgment, how can we expect to be perfect? After their failures, however, they repented, prayed and returned to God. That is exactly what any married couple should do when they find they are out of sync with God's rules. Ask for forgiveness from God, and from your spouse, and begin obeying God's rules for happiness.

It is never too late to start following God's eight basic rules. Try it and you will find a sense of security and happiness in your marriage, exceeding your wildest dreams.

You will be drawn closer to your spouse than you ever imagined, and it will be evident in every aspect of your relationship. The knot will not be broken. God has promised it, and God doesn't lie. Wedlock places a man and his wife in bonds, tied to one another, but they are not in bondage. Marriage is a beautiful thing.

THE END

www.ingramcontent.com/pod-product-compliance
Lightning Source LLC
Chambersburg PA
CBHW031234280526
45784CB00004B/1567